PRIMARY SCHOOL

Jumbo jets

Althea and Edward Parker
Illustrations by Peter Bailey

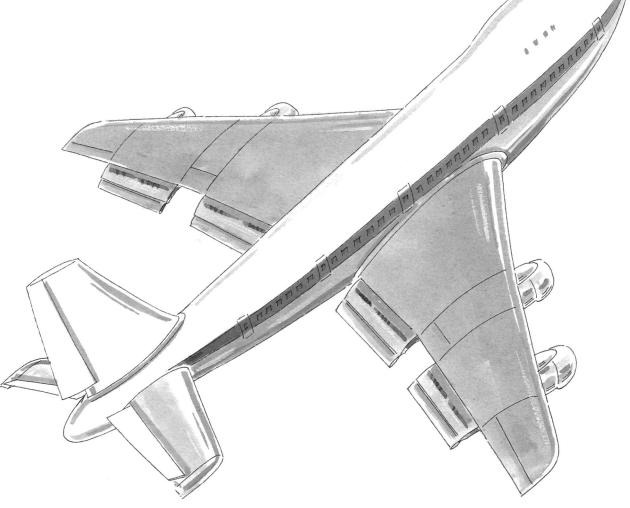

A & C Black · London

First published 1992
A & C Black (Publishers) Limited
35 Bedford Row, London WC1R 4JH

ISBN 0-7136-3535-5

© 1992, text, Althea and Edward Parker
© 1992, illustrations, Peter Bailey (Linda Rogers
Associates)

A CIP catalogue record for this book is
available from the British Library.

Acknowledgements
Edited by Barbara Taylor
Photographs by: Airbourne Halifax page 9; Alan Cork
page 17; Britannia Airways Limited page 21; M. J.
Hooks page 22; Civic Aviation Authority page 27;
Stan Elston Genus Publications page 31.

Photoset by Rowland Phototypesetting Limited
Bury St Edmunds, Suffolk
Printed in Italy by L.E.G.O. Spa.

Contents

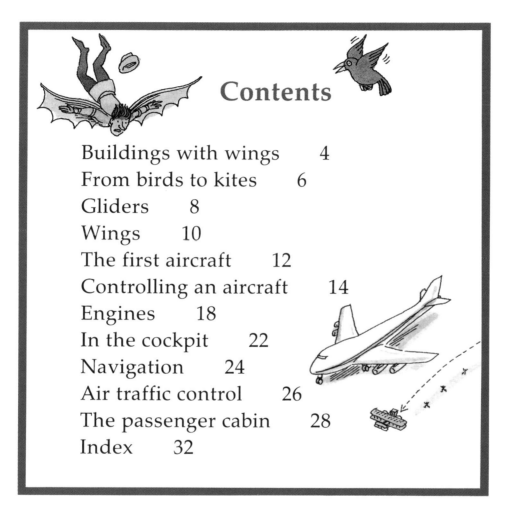

Buildings with wings

This is a small factory on an industrial estate. It is full of machines and lots of people work there. The factory has a kitchen and staff restaurant as well as toilets and washrooms. Heating and air conditioning systems keep people comfortable while they work. There is piped music and a public address system for announcements and the building is full of telephones and computers.

Now picture this building ten kilometres up in the air and hurtling along at 1000 kilometres per hour. Does this sound impossible?

The jumbo jet is like a building crammed full of complex machinery. Each one of its four huge engines produces a thrust of 15,000 kilograms (that's about as hard as you can blow multiplied by 300,000). It weighs over 300 tonnes, carries as much fuel as a fleet of 400 trucks and stands as high as a small block of flats. It can carry 400 people and keep them comfortable and fed on non-stop flights lasting up to fourteen hours.

It's hard to believe how big these machines are unless you stand under one. As the aircraft lands and the wheels touch the runway, the pilot in the cockpit is still 50 metres up in the air.

Although the jumbo looks very different from early wood and fabric aeroplanes, the engineering principles on which it is built and flies are very similar to the pioneering aircraft of a hundred years ago.

What a big nose!

From birds to kites

The idea of flying has fascinated people for centuries, and history is full of legends about flying. Nearly all of them involve gods and goddesses who were seen as bird-like creatures.

The bird-people legends came about because the only flying things our ancestors would have seen were the birds. When people made their first attempts at flying they tried to copy birds. There are many records of men strapping wings made of fabric, or even feathers, to their arms and jumping off towers madly flapping their arms. All of these attempts ended with the 'pilot' in a heap at the bottom of the tower. The lucky ones were only bruised but many of them were killed.

FEATHER FAILURE

One birdman thought his wings would have worked if he had used eagle feathers instead of chicken feathers.

I should have remembered that chickens can't fly very well.

Birds have evolved a very light body structure. They also have a complicated wing bone arrangement with very powerful wing muscles. It is technically very difficult to build a machine to copy this design but, even more important, it is technically not necessary. There is a much easier engineering solution to the problem of flight that does not involve flapping wings.

The first practical aircraft, which were based on a rigid, fixed wing, were kites. These were invented by the Chinese about 2500 years ago. The design was probably based on the inventor's observation of the way that large birds such as eagles glide with their wings held steady, using wind and air currents to keep themselves airborne. Kites large enough to carry a person were built.

They haven't got a clue.

It looks so easy when birds do it.

Gliders

I don't think steam engines are the answer.

The experience gained in designing kites led directly to the design of the first true aircraft, which were gliders.

Many designs of glider were tried, but one built by Sir George Caley in 1853 was the first practical machine. It had many of the design features of a modern aircraft, even though it looked very different.

The first glider, built by Sir George Caley.

Sir George's glider started a whole series of experiments during the rest of the 19th Century, including some early attempts at powered flight. A Frenchman, Alphonse Penard, flew a model aircraft very similar to Sir George Caley's, powered by a giant rubber band, but the first flight using an engine was made by another Frenchman, Clement Ader. His aircraft was powered by a steam engine. This flight only lasted a few seconds but it proved that powered flight was possible.

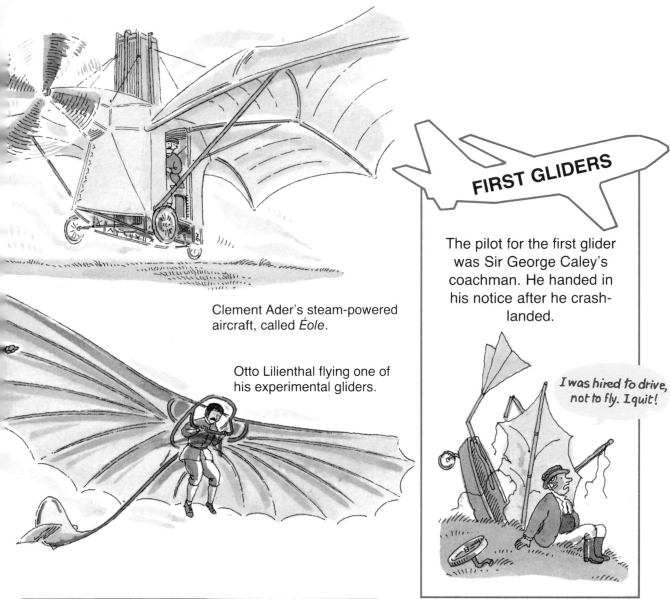

Clement Ader's steam-powered aircraft, called *Éole*.

Otto Lilienthal flying one of his experimental gliders.

FIRST GLIDERS

The pilot for the first glider was Sir George Caley's coachman. He handed in his notice after he crash-landed.

I was hired to drive, not to fly. I quit!

The shape of the wings of a modern hang-glider is based on Lilienthal's original designs.

Most of the basic problems of aircraft design and control in flight were solved by the German, Otto Lilienthal, who made hundreds of experiments with gliders between 1891 and 1896. Like so many pioneers of flight, Lilienthal crashed and was killed, but today's sport hang-gliders owe a lot to his experiments.

9

Wings

The things Lilienthal learned about wings were important to later designers who were able to make wing shapes which made the best use of a force called lift. This force is what keeps all aircraft up in the air and is the result of the way air flows over their wings.

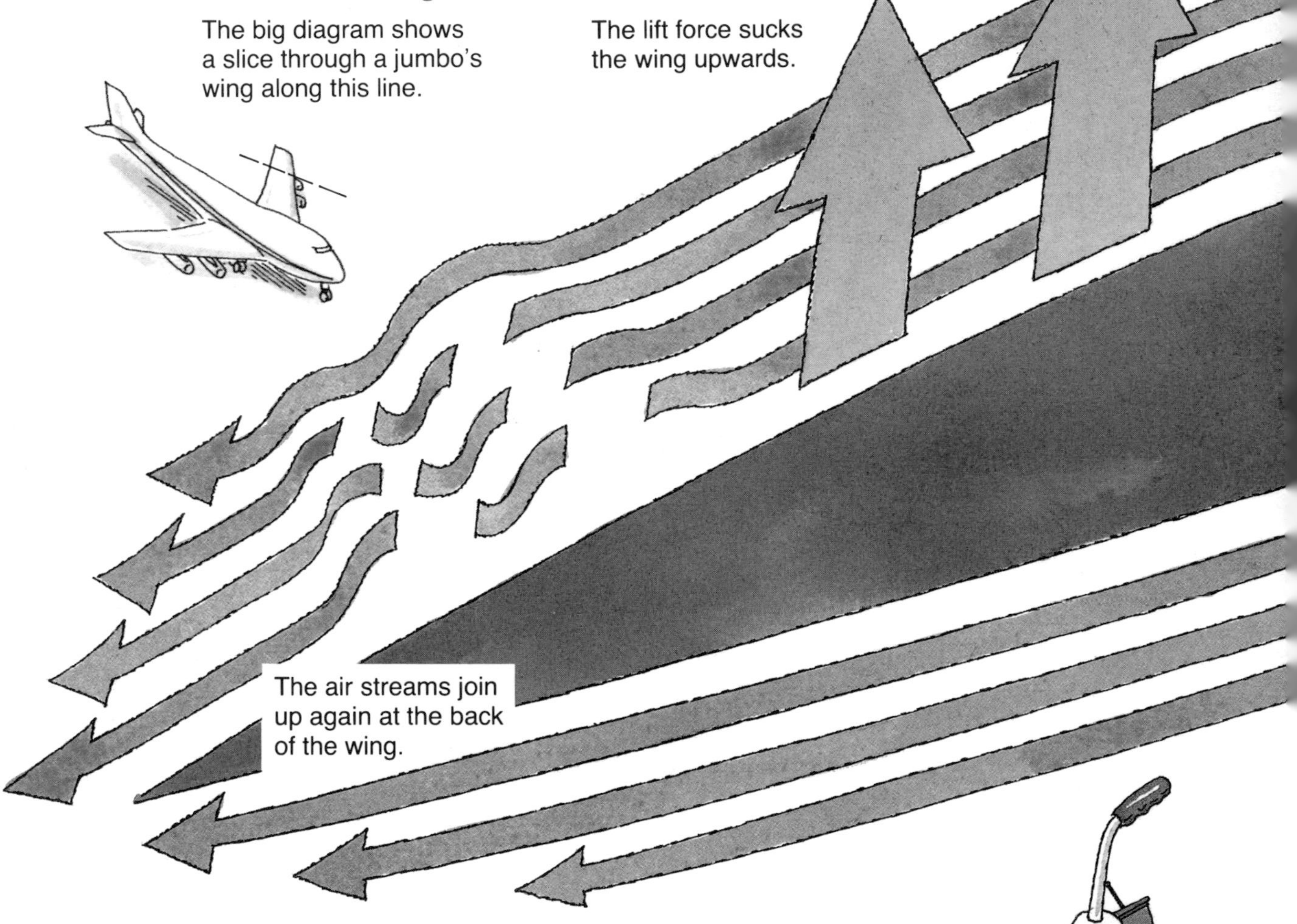

The big diagram shows a slice through a jumbo's wing along this line.

The lift force sucks the wing upwards.

The air streams join up again at the back of the wing.

A wing is shaped like a flattened tear drop with the fat end forwards. This shape is called an aerofoil. As the aircraft flies along, the wing splits the air stream in two, like a blunt knife going through butter. The wing is fixed to the aircraft at an angle with the back edge lower than the front. This slope, together with the tear drop shape of the wing, means that the air stream going over the top has further to go to get to the back edge of the wing than the underneath air stream. This means it is forced to move faster.

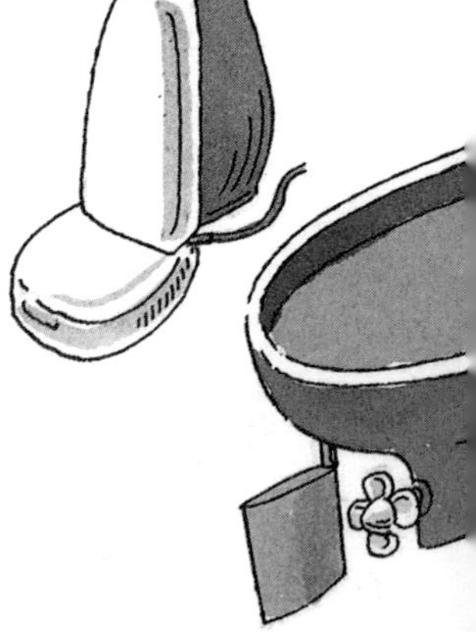

Fast-moving air on the top of the wing.

Low pressure

A law of physics says that the faster an air stream is moving, the lower its pressure is. Because of this, the faster-moving air on top of the wing is at a lower pressure than the slower moving air under the wing. This difference in pressure produces the lift, which sucks the aircraft's wing upwards in much the same way as you suck a drink up a straw.

Slower moving air underneath the wing.

They must get cold without feathers.

High pressure

If you blow over the top of a piece of paper, the paper lifts upwards. The air moving over an aircraft's wing lifts it up into the air in the same way.

Many things work in the same way as aircraft wings. Electric fans, ships' rudders, windmills, boat sails, turbine blades in engines, sycamore seeds and vacuum cleaners all contain aerofoil parts, which produce lift.

The amount of lift a wing produces depends on its speed through the air and the way it slopes downwards towards the back. Wings have to produce enough lift to support the weight of the aircraft and they have to do it over a range of speeds.

The first aircraft

One of the problems faced by designers of early aircraft was controlling the amount of lift. The other problem was being able to steer the aircraft and make it dive and climb.

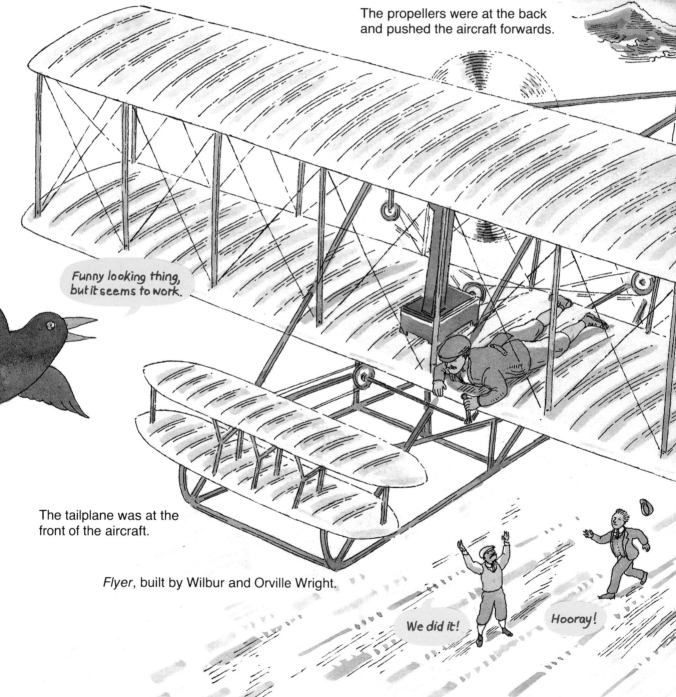

The propellers were at the back and pushed the aircraft forwards.

Funny looking thing, but it seems to work.

The tailplane was at the front of the aircraft.

Flyer, built by Wilbur and Orville Wright.

We did it!

Hooray!

A Vickers Vimy bomber made the first non-stop flight across the Atlantic Ocean on June 14th 1919. The flight took 16 hours.

The first practical powered aircraft was the *Flyer*, built by the American brothers Wilbur and Orville Wright at Kitty Hawk in North Carolina in 1903. *Flyer* had a lightweight petrol engine (like a car engine) which drove two propellers. By 1904, the Wright brothers could make long flights under complete control.

The design of aircraft developed very quickly after the Wrights' machine and by the end of the First World War, big aircraft with four engines were being built. The first passenger aircraft were wartime bombers with passenger cabins but they had all of the important design features of a modern passenger aircraft.

Handley Page HP42 airliners like this one were the most comfortable passenger aircraft of the 1930s. They were also the slowest, with a top speed of only 140 kilometres per hour.

Controlling an aircraft

Aircraft wings are designed so that the pilot can alter the angle of attack of the wing to suit his speed. This is done with small extra wings which can be hinged downwards at the back edge of the main wings. These 'flaps' make the wing slope downwards more at the back, producing more lift.

The flaps in a jumbo's wing are extended during take-off and landing to produce extra lift when the aircraft is flying slowly. When the aircraft has reached its normal flying speed, the flaps are slid back into the wing.

The wings, tailplane and tail fin all have small movable parts called 'control surfaces'. The ones on the wing are called 'ailerons', the tailplane has 'elevators', and the tail fin has a rudder. They all work like small wings and allow the pilot to make the aircraft turn, climb or dive.

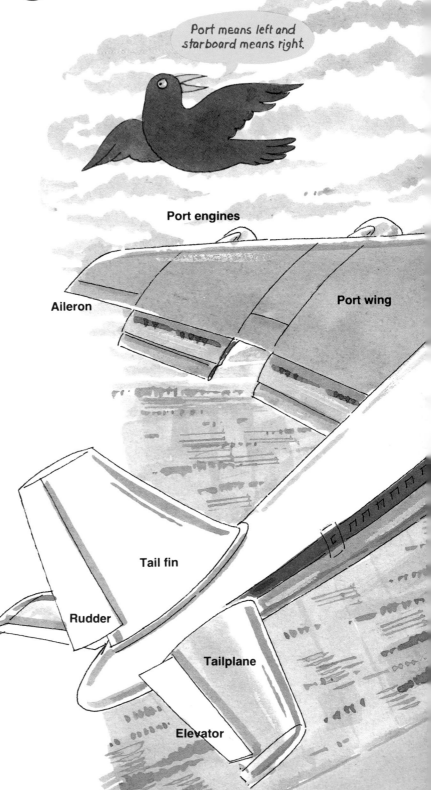

Port means left and starboard means right.

Port engines

Port wing

Aileron

Tail fin

Rudder

Tailplane

Elevator

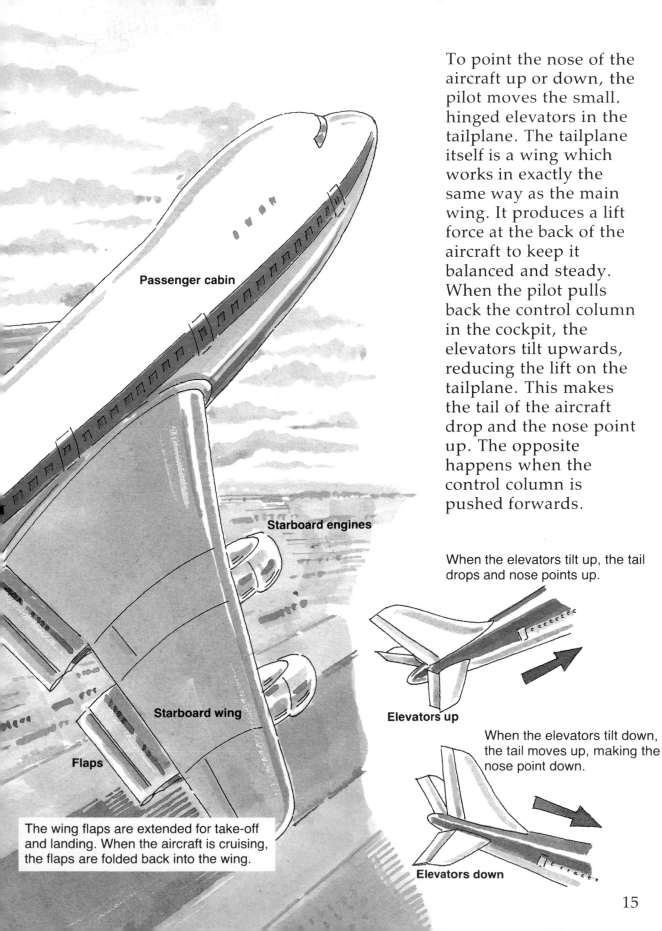

To point the nose of the aircraft up or down, the pilot moves the small, hinged elevators in the tailplane. The tailplane itself is a wing which works in exactly the same way as the main wing. It produces a lift force at the back of the aircraft to keep it balanced and steady. When the pilot pulls back the control column in the cockpit, the elevators tilt upwards, reducing the lift on the tailplane. This makes the tail of the aircraft drop and the nose point up. The opposite happens when the control column is pushed forwards.

Passenger cabin

Starboard engines

Starboard wing

Flaps

The wing flaps are extended for take-off and landing. When the aircraft is cruising, the flaps are folded back into the wing.

When the elevators tilt up, the tail drops and nose points up.

Elevators up

When the elevators tilt down, the tail moves up, making the nose point down.

Elevators down

15

The tail fin and rudder work in the same way as the wing. But because the fin is vertical, the lift forces push the tail of the aircraft from side to side instead of up and down.

The rudder works together with the ailerons on the wings. These work the opposite way round on each wing so that as one moves downwards, the other moves upwards. The ailerons are used to help turn the aircraft by tilting or 'banking' it to the side the rudder is set to turn it.

To turn left, the pilot pushes the left rudder bar with his foot, which turns the rudder to the left. The lift forces on the tail fin and rudder then push the tail of the aircraft to the right so that the nose starts to point left. At the same time, the pilot turns the wheel on the control column to the left.

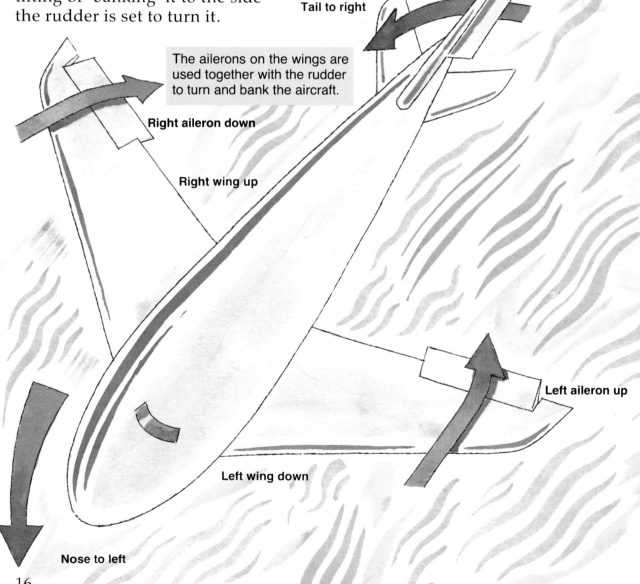

The rudder pushes the tail from side to side to turn the aircraft.

Tail to right

Rudder to left

The ailerons on the wings are used together with the rudder to turn and bank the aircraft.

Right aileron down

Right wing up

Left aileron up

Left wing down

Nose to left

Control surfaces and flaps on the wings can be moved to change the shape of the wings.

Birds fly and control themselves in a very similar way except that they use their wings for both lift and drive. Aircraft designers aren't quite as clever as birds and have to use separate wings and engines. The closest we can get to the way birds fly is with the helicopter. The spinning rotor is both a wing producing lift and a propeller giving driving thrust.

Helicopters are the closest they've come to the way I do it.

The spinning rotor blades of a helicopter are like wings, producing lift. They are also tilted slightly forwards to make a driving force like a propeller.

The small rotor blades on the tail keep the helicopter stable and stop it spinning round.

Engines

The jumbo and most modern aircraft have gas turbine engines. The main parts of this type of engine are the compressor at the front, the combustion chambers where the fuel is burnt and the turbine wheel which produces the power to drive the compressor. Aircraft gas turbine engines give a driving force or 'thrust' with a fast-moving jet of air and hot gases.

The compressor is a series of fans which suck air into the front of the engine. It works in a similar way to a vacuum cleaner, sucking air in one end and blowing it out the other end. The compressor in a gas turbine engine forces the air it sucks in into a combustion chamber behind the compressor. Kerosene fuel is pumped into the combustion chamber from a ring of nozzles and mixes with the stream of compressed air.

The compressor works like a vacuum cleaner, sucking air in one end and blowing it out the other end.

The compressor sucks cold air into the front of the engine and squeezes it into the combustion chambers.

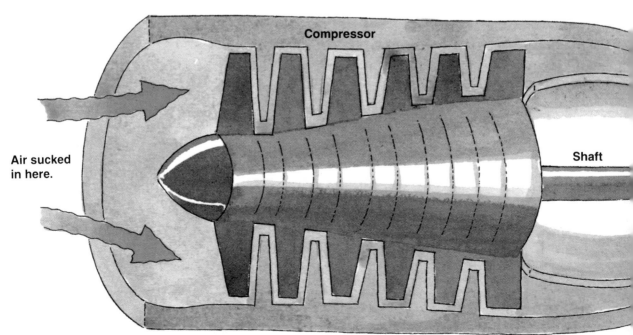

Compressor

Air sucked in here.

Shaft

The fuel and air mixture burns with very hot and fierce flames, which come from each of the fuel nozzles like giant blowtorches. The hot air and gas from these flames expands out from the combustion chambers and blasts through the turbine wheel.

The turbine wheel is like a windmill, and the blades on the turbine wheel are like a series of small sails. The hot, expanding gases from the burning fuel and compressed air coming in the front are like an extremely powerful wind which drives the turbine wheel round. The turbine wheel and the compressor are connected by shafts so the power produced by the turbine drives the compressor fans.

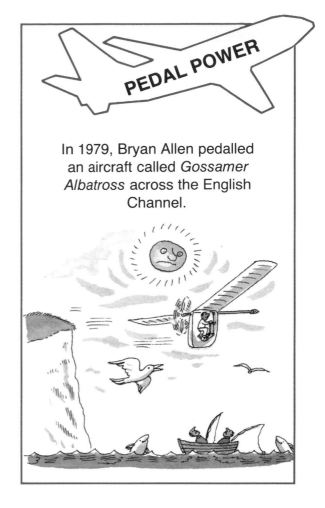

PEDAL POWER

In 1979, Bryan Allen pedalled an aircraft called *Gossamer Albatross* across the English Channel.

The turbine wheel is like a windmill, driven round by the 'wind' of hot gases from the combustion chambers.

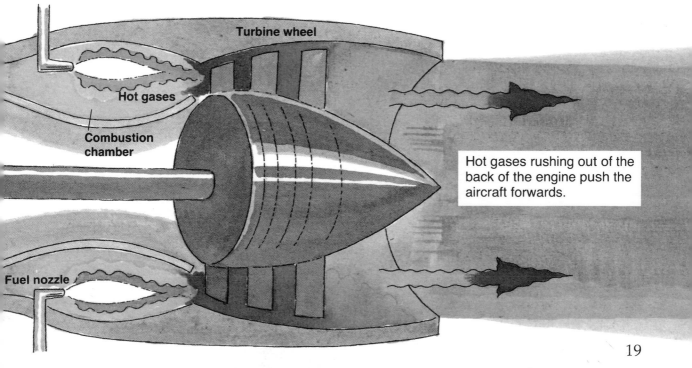

Turbine wheel

Hot gases

Combustion chamber

Fuel nozzle

Hot gases rushing out of the back of the engine push the aircraft forwards.

After going through the turbine wheel, the hot exhaust gases rush out in a jet from the wide nozzle at the back of the engine and push the aircraft forwards. The same thing happens when you let go of a balloon and it shoots around the room as the air rushes out.

Engineers are checking over this aircraft very carefully to make sure all the machinery is working safely and efficiently.

The jumbo has a particular type of gas turbine engine called a turbofan. In this engine, some of the power from the turbine, as well as driving the compressor, drives a huge fan at the front of the engine. The big fan forces a jet of fast-moving air backwards through a big tube around the engine. This 'bypass' jet joins up with the turbine exhaust gases at the back of the engine and adds to the power of the driving jet. The engines on the jumbo actually produce most of their driving thrust from this bypass jet. Most of the power from the turbine is used up in driving the compressor and fan and the exhaust jet gives only about one third of the total thrust of the engine.

This diagram shows how a turbofan engine works.

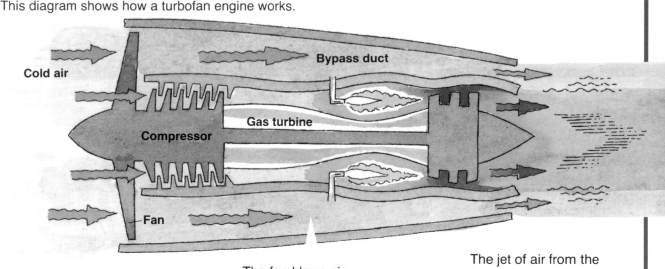

Cold air

Bypass duct

Compressor

Gas turbine

Fan

The fan blows air through this big tube around the gas turbine.

The jet of air from the fan mixes with the jet of gases from the turbine and adds to the thrust of the engine.

It's got to be ready for next Tuesday.

Turbofan engines are used on jumbos because these engines can be made powerful enough to produce the high thrust needed to drive a big aircraft. At the same time, they are fairly quiet because the bypass jet cools and muffles the loud noise of the turbine exhaust. This is important because airports are usually close to houses and airline companies have to obey strict regulations about noise pollution. Turbofans are also efficient and burn fuel economically. Engine designers are constantly trying to improve engines to make them less polluting to the atmosphere.

This photograph shows you how big the engines on a jumbo really are. Can you see the huge fan at the front of the engine?

In the cockpit

If you sit in a pilot's seat in the cockpit of a jumbo, you are faced with a mass of dials, switches, gauges, levers, lights, knobs and screens. It all looks very complicated but it is similar to a car dashboard and does the same job. A lot of the dials and gauges monitor the performance of the engines and record things like fuel consumption, combustion chamber pressures, exhaust jet temperatures and engine revolutions. Other instruments allow the pilots to keep a check on all the other machinery in the aircraft so they know that everything is working properly.

Beside the pilots' seats are switches to control things such as cabin lights, and the throttle levers which control the power of the engines. Some of the instruments do the important job of giving the pilots information about the speed and height of the aircraft which they use to find their way around or 'navigate'.

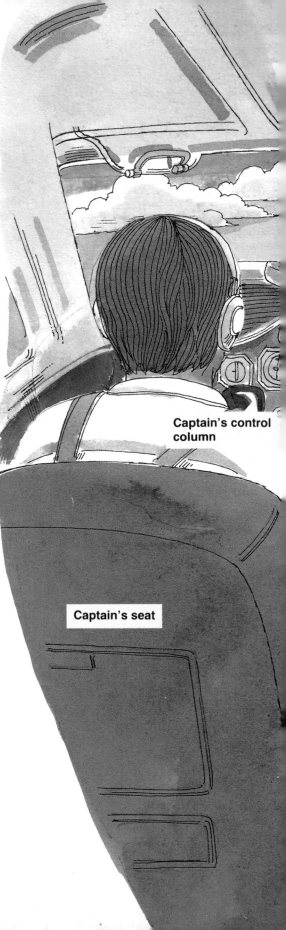

Captain's control column

Captain's seat

In the future, more jumbo jets will have cockpits like this one, with electronic instruments instead of some of the gauges and switches.

22

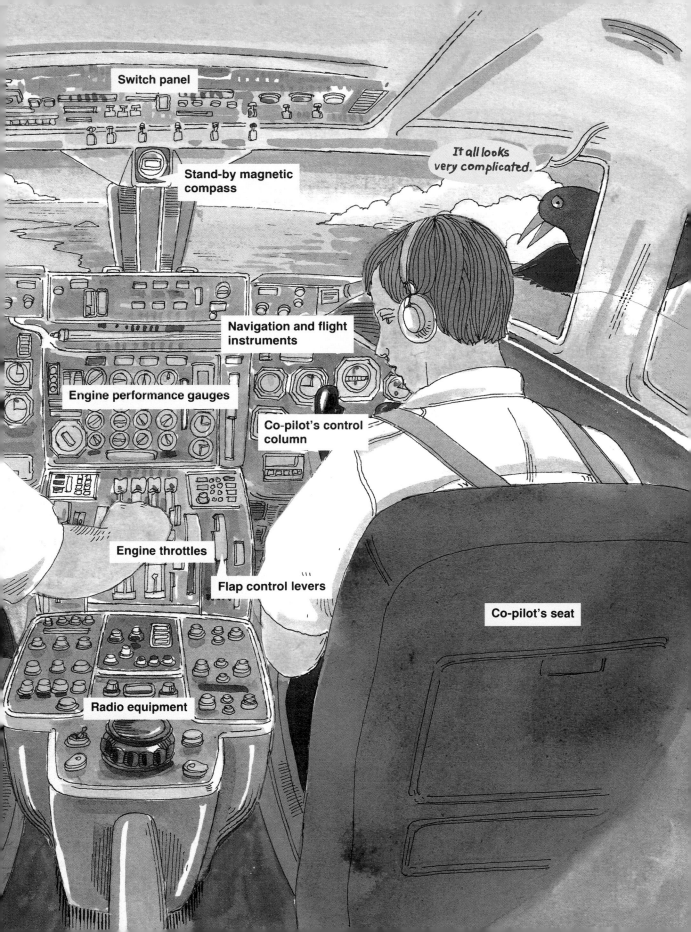

Radio transmitter beacon

As the aircraft flies over the chain of radio beacons, the navigation equipment in the cockpit measures the signals and calculates the position of the aircraft.

Navigation

The jumbo has three kinds of navigation equipment. It has an ordinary compass with a needle which points to the Earth's North magnetic pole. The pilots can plot their course with this and use charts and take sightings of stars to calculate the aircraft's position. They would only do this in an emergency though if the other navigation systems went wrong.

The main navigational system uses signals picked up by the aircraft from a chain of radio beacons like 'radio lighthouses'. The aircraft's electronics or 'avionics' use these signals to calculate the aircraft's position as it flies from beacon to beacon.

If I had one of those, I wouldn't get lost in the fog.

Radio beams

The third important part of the navigational equipment is called inertial guidance. This is an electronic and mechanical device which can 'remember' the details of an airport, such as where it is and its height above sea level. When the aircraft takes off, all its movements, speeds, directions and the length of time it has been flying are recorded by the system. It keeps a kind of electronic map inside itself and 'knows' where the aircraft is all the time in relation to the airport it took off from.

Aircraft also have an electronic system called ILS which uses radio signals transmitted from an airport to guide the aircraft to a safe landing even in fog and bad weather. In the latest aircraft, this equipment is computer-controlled and aircraft can, and do, fly and land themselves automatically.

WHICH WAY?

To find their way around, pilots of the early aircraft had to fly low enough to read road signs or follow railway tracks. Sometimes they even had to land to ask for directions.

THIS WAY

Radio signals from marker transmitters near the airport show the distance of the aircraft from the runway.

The electronic ILS system in the cockpit uses radio beams from transmitters at the end of the runway to keep the aircraft in the right position for landing.

Runway

Radio signal

Air traffic control

Behind the engine controls in the cockpit is the radio communications equipment that the crew uses to talk to the aircraft controllers on the ground. These people, called 'air traffic control', keep a watch on all the aircraft taking off and landing at their airport. They have big radar screens which show the positions of all the aircraft in the sky around them.

The skies are so crowded these days.

The air traffic controllers talk to the pilots with the radio telephone.

The radio is very important because modern airports are usually very busy and aircraft may be arriving and taking off within minutes of each other. The sky around an airport is very crowded. The pilots have radar to warn them of other aircraft around them but they rely on the ground controllers. Air traffic controllers give the pilots instructions about how high they should be, and how fast they should be going, as the aircraft approaches the runway.

Communication between the pilot and the ground is much more important than in the early days of flying. Modern aircraft fly very fast and big aircraft like the jumbo need a lot of airspace to move around in. Two aircraft which are 10 kilometres apart are only a few seconds apart in time if they are heading towards each other.

Air traffic control desks like this one control the movement of aircraft in and out of airports.

The passenger cabin

The most important parts of a jumbo, apart from all the complicated machinery and the crew are, of course, the passenger cabins. Moving people from one place to another, quickly and comfortably, is the job of a big passenger aircraft.

The main passenger cabin, or fuselage, of all modern aircraft is a long tube made from aluminium alloys. An alloy is a mixture of different metals. Aircraft builders use alloys of aluminium, copper and zinc to make strong and light girders and frames. The fuselage of a jumbo is a bit like a basket made of circular frames joined by girders, with a thin metal skin riveted to it. The wings and tail are made in the same way and fixed to the main fuselage with giant bolts.

Circular frames

Cockpit

Deck girders

The baggage is stored under the passenger cabin.

Radar equipment

The fuselage and the wings are quite flexible and, if you fly in a jumbo, you will see the ends of the wings moving up and down. This is part of the design and allows the aircraft to flex and twist to resist the buffeting it gets from winds and the air rushing over it.

The inside wall of the cabin is covered by plastic panels which hide the mass of wiring and pipes.

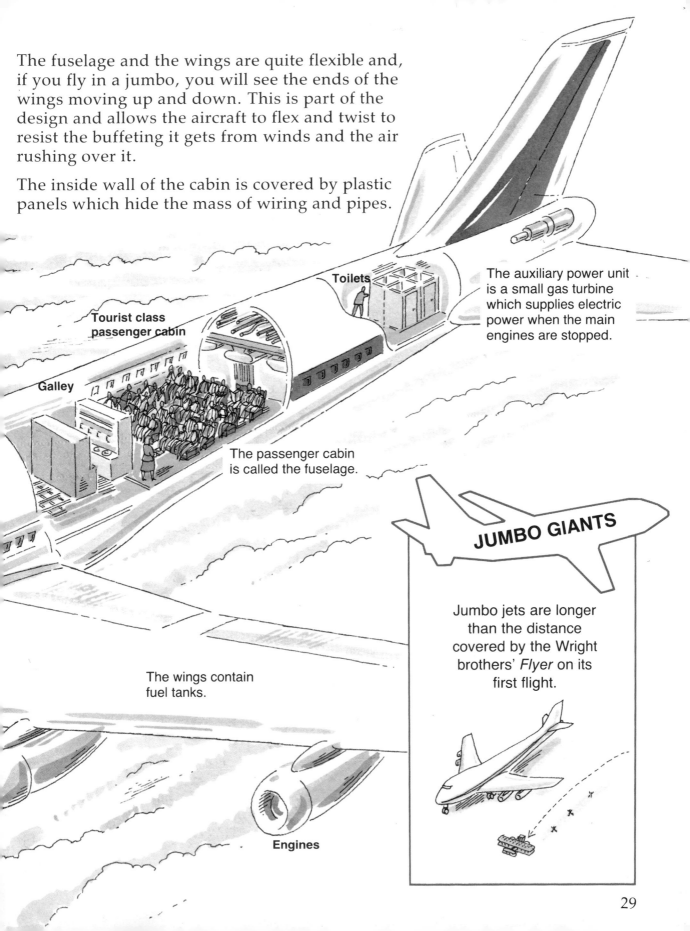

Toilets

Tourist class passenger cabin

The auxiliary power unit is a small gas turbine which supplies electric power when the main engines are stopped.

Galley

The passenger cabin is called the fuselage.

JUMBO GIANTS

Jumbo jets are longer than the distance covered by the Wright brothers' *Flyer* on its first flight.

The wings contain fuel tanks.

Engines

The first page of this book compared the jumbo to a small factory. Its engines drive electric generators to make power for lighting, heating and cooking and the aircraft has most of the things you would expect to find in a building on the ground. One important thing you would expect to find is air to breathe.

A jumbo flies at a height where the pressure of the atmosphere is so low that it would be impossible to breath in enough oxygen to stay alive. Because of this, the passenger cabin of a jumbo is pressurised. Pumps, driven by the engines, suck in air from the outside and pump it into the passenger cabin just like blowing air into a balloon.

The air pressure in the cabin is kept at a level which people find comfortable but which is about half the pressure on the ground. It is kept lower because an aircraft which could be pumped up to ground air pressure would have to be built much stronger and heavier.

As you sit in your seat, eating hot food served by the cabin staff, listening to music, watching a film or leaving your seat to go to a toilet, it is sometimes difficult to believe that you are travelling in a big aircraft far above the clouds.

The large size of the jumbo makes it ideal for carrying heavy freight and some jumbos are built as cargo aircraft. They look very different to the passenger jumbos because they don't have any cabin windows and the nose opens like a huge mouth to load the cargo aboard.

The aircraft pioneers, if they could be sitting with you, would be pleased, although probably not very surprised. They would be happy that their dream of flight had come so spectacularly true.

Index